ClassiChoice

Classichoice
Handwriting Series:

Handwriting Is Fun - Book 1

Written, edited and designed by Classichoice, LLC.

ISBN: 9781792901942

About This Book

The **Classichoice Handwriting Series** is designed to practice handwriting through fun exercises. **Handwriting Is Fun - Book 1** consists of handwriting exercises for 200 vocabulary words encountered from academic and practical life. We placed the words into several topics, including months & seasons, transportation, colors, feelings, sports, food, and human body.

We have broken down the immense task of practicing handwriting into manageable, enjoyable units. We truly believe that each student will grow in confidence and a love of handwriting as he/she masters each unit.

How to Use This Book

We have 25 different topics in this book. Each topic consists of 4 units and introduces 8 vocabulary words, using the following format:

- The first and second units of each topic introduce 4 words each and allow the student to practice writing the words.

- The third and fourth units of each topic allow the student to practice writing the words in sentences.

About Us

Classichoice Books began with a group of parents' desire to keep their own children engaged in their learning journey at home and away from school. Since its initial book of sight words for kindergarteners, **Classichoice** has expanded to include books from kindergarten level to fifth grade in areas including vocabulary, handwriting, reading, language, and math and word search books for both kids and adults. The **Classichoice** authors, under the leadership of co-founders Sean McCann and Emmy McCann, continue to strive to incorporate instructional materials and activities that will bring students success in the classroom and beyond.

Sean McCann, M.A. Ed., is an author, educational consultant, and a certified teacher with over two decades of classroom experience in New York City. He trains teachers in staff development workshops, develops curriculum, and teaches diverse groups of children. With a specific expertise in science and literacy, Sean has been recently selected as a STEM Teacher-Scholar at Columbia University in New York City.

Emmy McCann, M.B.A., is an author and educational consultant with classroom experiences on three continents, including Europe, Asia, and the U. S. With a Wall Street background in finance and school district administrative experience, she has developed an interest and expertise in both literacy and math for young children.

Table of Contents

1 Academic Words
School Supplies

crayon

glue

paint

paper

2 **Academic Words**
School Supplies

pen

pencil

scissors

tape

3

Sentences with
School Supplies words

• He used scissors to cut

holes in the paper.

• She had blue paint on

her shirt and pants after

art class.

Sentences with
School Supplies words

- Please use tape or

glue to join the pieces.

- His crayon box has

pens and colored

pencils.

5

Practical Life Words
Family Members

father

mother

brother

sister

Practical Life Words
Family Members

son

daughter

uncle

aunt

7

Sentences with
Family Members words

• My father has a

younger brother.

• My mother and her

sister are talking on the

phone.

8

Sentences with
Family Members words

• My aunt has a son and

a daughter.

• My uncle Fred likes to

tell us great stories

every time we see him.

Practical Life Words
Transportation

bicycle

boat

bus

car

10 **Practical Life Words**
Transportation

tire

tractor

train

truck

11

Sentences with
Transportation words

• He changed the tire

of his bicycle.

• The cars and buses

waited for the train to

pass.

Sentences with
Transportation words

• The boats were

passing on the river.

• The farmer used both

his truck and tractor

in the field.

13 **Academic Words**
Farm Animals

calf

cow

donkey

goat

14 **Academic Words**
Farm Animals

horse

lamb

pig

sheep

15

Sentences with
Farm Animals words

• The horse is bigger

than the donkey.

• The calf, lamb and

the sheep are good

friends.

16 **Sentences** with
Farm Animals words

- Be careful around the

group of goats.

- We saw many cows

and pigs on the farm

yesterday.

Practical Life Words
Body Parts

chest

ear

eye

finger

18 **Practical Life Words**
Body Parts

nose

stomach

throat

toe

19 **Sentences** with
Body Parts words

• His fingers and toes

were cold.

• My brother is sick and

has a runny nose and

stomach ache.

20 **Sentences** with Body Parts words

• Her doctor checked

her eyes, ears, throat,

and chest during the

physical exam

yesterday.

21

Practical Life Words
Body Parts

arm
_____
- - - - - - - - - - - - - - - -
_____

face
_____
- - - - - - - - - - - - - - - -
_____

feet
_____
- - - - - - - - - - - - - - - -
_____

hair
_____
- - - - - - - - - - - - - - - -
_____

22 **Practical Life Words**
Body Parts

heart

leg

mouth

tooth

23 | **Sentences** with
Body Parts words

• My legs and feet are

sore from running.

• His heart pumped fast,

and his face turned red

during the race.

24

Sentences with
Body Parts words

• Wipe your mouth and

brush your teeth now.

• I need to brush my

hair.

• He broke his arm.

General Words
Feelings

25

afraid

glad

grumpy

happy

26 **General Words**
Feelings

mad

sad

shy

silly

Sentences with
Feelings words

- I'm afraid of grumpy,

large dogs.

- Are you mad or glad

about school being

cancelled?

28 **Sentences** with Feelings words

- I can tell a silly joke.

- I usually don't like sad

stories with no happy

endings.

- My dog is very shy.

Practical Life Words
Days

Monday

Tuesday

Wednesday

Thursday

Practical Life Words
Days

Friday

Saturday

Sunday

weekend

Sentences with
Days words

• I have tests on

Monday and Tuesday.

• I have soccer practice

on Wednesday and

Thursday this week.

32 **Sentences** with Days words

• I want to relax on

Friday evening.

• Saturday and Sunday

are the days of the

weekend.

33 **Academic Words**
In the School

art

book

class

library

34 **Academic Words**
In the School

music

_____

- - - - - - - - - - - -

_____

song

_____

- - - - - - - - - - - -

_____

teach

_____

- - - - - - - - - - - -

_____

voice

_____

- - - - - - - - - - - -

_____

35

Sentences with
In the School words

• I returned all my books

to the library.

• Our art instructor

teaches us different

ways to paint.

36   **Sentences** with
In the School words

• We sang songs during

music class today.

• The students use their

beautiful voices in

choir.

37

Practical Life Words
Months & Seasons

January

February

March

April

38 **Practical Life Words**
Months & Seasons

May

June

winter

spring

39

Sentences with
Months & Seasons words

• We can build

snowmen in the winter.

• The weather is usually

very cold during

January and February.

Sentences with
Months & Seasons words

• In New York, the

months of March, April,

May, and June make up

the spring, when flowers

and trees bloom.

41 **Practical Life Words**
Months & Seasons

July
_____

August
_____

September
_____

October
_____

Practical Life Words
Months & Seasons

November

December

summer

fall

Sentences with
Months & Seasons words

• We go on vacation

during July and August

and return to school in

September.

• I hike in the summer.

44

Sentences with
Months & Seasons words

• In the fall, we go

pumpkin picking during

October or November.

• December is the last

month of the year.

45

Academic Words
Wild Animals

bear

bird

elephant

giraffe

46

Academic Words
Wild Animals

lion

monkey

tiger

zebra

Sentences with
Wild Animals words

• Elephants and giraffes

are big animals from

Africa.

• Lions and zebras are

enemies in the wild.

48

Sentences with
Wild Animals words

• We saw monkeys,

bears, and tigers at the

zoo.

• You could hear the

birds singing here.

49

Practical Life Words
Time of Day

afternoon

evening

morning

night

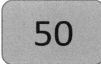 **Practical Life Words**
Time of Day

today

tomorrow

tonight

yesterday

51 **Sentences** with Time of Day words

- I have my dance

recital tomorrow

afternoon.

- It rained a lot

yesterday evening.

52

Sentences with
Time of Day words

- Today, I took a bath

at night.

- I will study tonight.

- I ate cereal in the

morning.

Practical Life Words
Furniture

53

bed

chair

desk

lamp

54 **Practical Life Words**
Furniture

mirror

rug

table

window

55 **Sentences** with Furniture words

- I think I left my key

either on my desk or

bed.

- The lamp reflected its

light in the mirror.

Sentences with
Furniture words

- He loves to sit in a

chair next to the

window.

- The table was placed

on the rug.

57 **General Words**
Actions

correct

dry

hear

hug

58

General Words
Actions

hurry

listen

scratch

speak

| 59 | **Sentences** with Actions words |

• Don't scratch the wall

because the paint is

still drying.

• I hear my dad

correcting my sister.

60

Sentences with
Actions words

• I like to hug my mom.

• Hurry up before it

rains.

• Listen to the teacher

when she is speaking.

61 **Practical Life Words**
Clothing

boots

coat

dress

hat

62 **Practical Life Words**
Clothing

pants

shirt

shoes

socks

63 **Sentences** with
Clothing words

• We wear boots, hats,

and coats when it's

cold in the winter.

• I can dress myself

without any help.

Sentences with
Clothing words

• You need to wear a

polo shirt and pants to

school.

• I put on my socks and

shoes last.

65 | **Academic Words**
Colors

brown

green

red

orange

66

Academic Words
Colors

pink

violet

white

yellow

67 **Sentences** with
Colors words

• A yellow light from the

sun shined through the

white clouds.

• The flower has violet

and pink petals.

68 **Sentences** with
Colors words

• My lawn is green in

the spring but turns

brown by the summer.

• Orange and red are

my favorite colors.

69

Academic Words
Color & Shade

black

blue

bright

dark

70

Academic Words
Color & Shade

gray

light

purple

rainbow

71

Sentences with
Color & Shade words

• The light red birds flew

through the bright, blue

sky.

• I love my beautiful

purple dress.

Sentences with
Color & Shade words

• The forest turned to

dark black at night.

• The rainbow began to

show through the gray

clouds.

73 **Practical Life Words**
Sports

ball

bat

camp

climb

74 **Practical Life Words**
Sports

dance

game

race

swim

Sentences with
Sports words

75

- She has always loved

to dance.

- He hit the ball very far

with the bat during the

game.

76

Sentences with
Sports words

- He swims his fastest

during races.

- During our camping

trip, we climbed the

mountain.

77 **Practical Life Words**
Food

cereal

egg

jelly

juice

78 **Practical Life Words**
Food

milk

pizza

snack

soup

79   **Sentences** with Food words

• For her breakfast, she

has cereal with milk,

eggs, a peanut butter

and jelly sandwich, and

orange juice.

80 **Sentences** with Food words

• I put a small snack in

my bag.

• We will have

vegetable soup and

pizza for dinner.

<table>
<tr><td>81</td><td>**Practical Life Words**
Fruits</td></tr>
</table>

apple

banana

blueberry

cherry

82 **Practical Life Words**
Fruits

fruit

peach

strawberry

watermelon

83 **Sentences** with Fruits words

• I have an apple or

banana as a snack.

• We grow strawberries

and watermelons in our

garden.

84 — **Sentences** with Fruits words

- Blueberry is my

favorite fruit.

- Would you prefer

cherry pie or peach

cobbler for dessert?

85 **Practical Life Words**
Dessert & Sweets

cake

----

candy

----

chips

----

cookie

86

Practical Life Words
Dessert & Sweets

cupcake

donut

ice cream

popcorn

87 **Sentences** with
Dessert & Sweets words

• The students were

selling cookies, donuts,

and cupcakes at the

bake sale.

• I love ice cream!

88

Sentences with
Dessert & Sweets words

• Would you prefer

popcorn, candy, or

chips for a snack?

• I ate a chocolate

cake.

89

Academic Words
Pet Animals

cat

dog

fish

frog

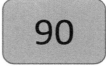

Academic Words
Pet Animals

goldfish

kitten

mouse

rabbit

91

Sentences with
Pet Animals words

- I wonder if all fish

live in the water.

- Frogs can jump high.

- A young cat is called

a kitten.

92

Sentences with
Pet Animals words

• I think I would prefer

a goldfish over a mouse

as a pet.

• The dog is chasing the

rabbit.

93 **General Words**
Adjectives

heavy

lazy

sick

slow

94

General Words
Adjectives

strong

thin

wet

wild

Sentences with
Adjective words

• The wet dog did not

want to dry off.

• The wild geese were

slow to eat food.

• My cat is very lazy.

96

Sentences with
Adjective words

• We had strong,

heavy winds all day

yesterday.

• We fed the sick and

thin stray cat.

97

Practical Life Words
Vacation in Nature

farm

lake

map

park

98

Practical Life Words
Vacation in Nature

pool

road

sea

town

99

Sentences with
Vacation in Nature words

• The town is located

near the sea.

• The park has a

swimming pool open to

all kids.

100

Sentences with
Vacation in Nature words

• The dirt road led us to

the animal farm.

• We needed to use a

map to find the route to

the lake.

Also available:

<u>Classichoice Vocabulary Series</u>
Top 300 Sight Words, Book 1 of 2
Top 300 Sight Words, Book 2 of 2
600 Essential Kindergarten Words, Book 1 of 3
600 Essential Kindergarten Words, Book 2 of 3
600 Essential Kindergarten Words, Book 3 of 3
Math & Science Words For K-1
My Home & Friends Words For K-1
Animal World Words For K-1

<u>Classichoice Math Series</u>
Addition & Subtraction Under 10
Addition & Subtraction Under 20
Addition & Subtraction Under 50
Addition & Subtraction Under 100
Addition & Subtraction Word Problems
Multiplication Practice
Division Practice
Multiplication & Division Practice
Multiplication & Division Word Problems

<u>Classichoice Handwriting Series</u>
Handwriting Is Fun - Book 1
Handwriting Is Fun - Book 2
Handwriting Is Fun - Book 3
Handwriting Is Fun - Math & Science Edition
Handwriting Is Fun - Animal World Edition
Handwriting Is Fun - Home & Friends Edition

<u>Classichoice Word Search Series</u>
Christmas Joy, Large Print
Christmas Joy
Love & Romance
Escape to Ireland
New York City Adventure

<u>Classichoice Reading Series</u>

<u>Classichoice Spelling Series</u>